AF228554

TORONTO RAPTORS

BY PATRICK DONNELLY

SportsZone

An Imprint of Abdo Publishing
abdobooks.com

abdobooks.com

Published by Abdo Publishing, a division of ABDO, PO Box 398166, Minneapolis, Minnesota 55439. Copyright © 2023 by Abdo Consulting Group, Inc. International copyrights reserved in all countries. No part of this book may be reproduced in any form without written permission from the publisher. SportsZone™ is a trademark and logo of Abdo Publishing.

Printed in China.
052022
092022

Cover Image: Michael Reaves/Getty Images Sport/Getty Images
Interior Photos: Melinda Nagy/Shutterstock Images, 1; Ezra Shaw/Getty Images Sport/Getty Images, 4, 9; Rick Madonik/Toronto Star/Getty Images, 7, 17, 40; Vaughn Ridley/Getty Images Sport/Getty Images, 8, 18, 26; Lachlan Cunningham/Getty Images Sport/Getty Images, 11; Carlo Allegri/AFP/Getty Images, 12; Harry How/Allsport/Getty Images Sport/Getty Images, 15; Mark Blinch/Getty Images Sport/Getty Images, 19; Doug Pensinger/Allsport/Getty Images Sport/Getty Images, 20; The Sporting News/Getty Images, 22, 23; Elsa/Getty Images Sport/Getty Images, 25; Frank Gunn/The Canadian Press/AP Images, 29; Andy Lyons/Allsport/Getty Images Sport/Getty Images, 30; Jed Jacobsohn/Allsport/Getty Images Sport/Getty Images, 33, 34; Aaron Harris/AFP/Getty Images, 37

Editor: Charlie Beattie
Series Designer: Joshua Olson

Library of Congress Control Number: 2021951661

Publisher's Cataloging-in-Publication Data

Names: Donnelly, Patrick, author.
Title: Toronto Raptors / by Patrick Donnelly
Description: Minneapolis, Minnesota: Abdo Publishing, 2023 | Series: Inside the NBA | Includes online resources and index.
Identifiers: ISBN 9781532198458 (lib. bdg.) | ISBN 9781098272104 (ebook)
Subjects: LCSH: Toronto Raptors (Basketball team)--Juvenile literature. | Basketball--Juvenile literature. | Professional sports--Juvenile literature. | Sports franchises--Juvenile literature.
Classification: DDC 796.32364--dc23

TABLE OF **CONTENTS**

GIANT KILLERS

The Toronto Raptors had already beaten the odds twice in the 2019 National Basketball Association (NBA) playoffs. Entering the Finals against the heavily favored Golden State Warriors, Toronto was ready to do it again.

The Raptors had never appeared in the NBA Finals before. By contrast, the Warriors were playing in their fifth straight championship series. They'd won three of them, including each of the last two years. Golden State was looking to become the first team to win three straight since the Los Angeles Lakers had done it in the early 2000s.

The Raptors had spent much of their 24-year existence hanging out near the bottom of the standings. And even when they'd had good teams, they hadn't done much in the postseason.

Kawhi Leonard averaged team highs of 30.5 points and 9.1 rebounds for the Raptors in the 2019 NBA playoffs.

However, this was a different Raptors team. Point guard Kyle Lowry was in his thirteenth NBA season. He'd played in his share of big games along the way. Center Marc Gasol, forward Serge Ibaka, and guard Danny Green were seasoned veterans too. They were ready for anything the Warriors could throw at them.

The heartbeat of the team was forward Kawhi Leonard. He had been to the NBA Finals twice with the San Antonio Spurs before coming to Toronto. He was even named Most Valuable Player (MVP) of the 2014 Finals when the Spurs knocked off the Miami Heat. Now he was one of the league's best players. Toronto's general manager Masai Ujiri had traded popular star DeMar DeRozan to bring Leonard to the Raptors as the missing piece.

ROAD TO THE FINALS

The Raptors finished the 2018–19 regular season 58–24. They won the Atlantic Division title and earned the second seed in the Eastern Conference playoffs. Their conference semifinal series versus the Philadelphia 76ers came down to the end of Game 7. Leonard hit a dramatic buzzer-beating jumper from the corner to win it for Toronto.

Perhaps worn out from the 76ers series, the Raptors lost the first two games of the conference finals against the top-seeded

Leonard, *right*, tries to rip the ball away from Milwaukee's Giannis Antetokounmpo during the 2019 Eastern Conference finals.

Milwaukee Bucks. But Leonard scored 36 points to turn the tide in Game 3. The Raptors won four straight to take the series.

Golden State had less stress on its road to the Finals. As the top seed in the West, the Warriors got the most out of their home-court advantage. They had just swept the Portland Trail Blazers in the Western Conference finals. But two-time NBA Finals MVP Kevin Durant had been injured during the run. The Warriors would have to start the Finals without the star forward.

TORONTO TAKES CONTROL

The Raptors had won one more game than Golden State during the regular season. As a result, the Finals opened in Toronto.

Toronto forward Pascal Siakam had a team-high 32 points in Game 1 of the 2019 NBA Finals.

The Raptors knew they had a size advantage against the run-and-gun Warriors. They used it early in Game 1. Gasol and power forward Pascal Siakam combined for 26 points in the first half as Toronto took a 10-point lead. The Raptors held on for a 118–109 win.

The Warriors bounced back in Game 2, however. Klay Thompson hit four three-pointers. Superstar guard Stephen Curry added 23 points to lead Golden State to a 109–104 win. Now the series shifted to Oakland, California, where Golden State was tough to beat. The Warriors had gone 30–11 at Oracle Arena during the regular season. They'd won six of their eight home playoff games, too.

Instead, the Raptors were dominant in Oakland. Leonard scored 30 points in a 123–109 victory in Game 3. Then Toronto took a 3–1 series lead as Leonard's 36 points paced a 105–92 win. The Raptors had a chance to close it out at home in Game 5. But Curry and Thompson hit back-to-back three-pointers to give the Warriors a 106–103 lead with just under a minute

to play. A Lowry basket cut the lead to a single point. Then Draymond Green blocked his three-pointer at the buzzer to send the series back to Oakland. But Game 5 wasn't all good news for Golden State. Durant, who had just returned from his earlier injury, tore his Achilles tendon.

CANADA CLINCHER

Emotions were running high as Game 6 began. Warriors fans certainly wanted to spur their banged-up team to victory. They were closing out Oracle Arena, the team's home since 1971. A new arena was set to open in San Francisco that fall. Lowry quieted the crowd by scoring the game's first eight points. His third straight three-pointer put Toronto on top 11–2.

The Warriors didn't back down. Midway through the second quarter, Draymond Green set up Andre Iguodala for two alley-oop dunks. The slams capped an 8–0 run that gave Golden State a three-point lead. Lowry responded with a sensational driving layup in the final minute to put Toronto up 60–57 at halftime.

The second half was more of the same. Neither team could pull away. The Warriors lost Thompson to a knee injury late in the third quarter. He had already scored 30 points on the night. On the other end, Siakam and Leonard were carrying the load, combining for 18 points in the third.

With less than four minutes to play in the fourth quarter, Toronto's Fred VanVleet hit his fifth three-pointer of the game. The shot put the Raptors up 104–101. Ibaka then scored on an offensive rebound to give Toronto some breathing room. Lowry banked in a jumper in traffic with the shot clock running out. Now Toronto was up by six. But the Warriors scored five straight to set up a hectic final minute.

Siakam hit a runner in the lane to give Toronto a 111–108 lead with 26 seconds to go. Curry answered with a pair of

The Raptors became the first team from outside of the United States to win an NBA title when they defeated the Warriors in 2019.

free throws. Then the Raptors threw the ball away, giving Golden State a chance to win it.

Curry got a look at a three-pointer, but the ball bounced off the rim. The rebound skittered through a sea of arms and legs. Draymond Green dived on the ball at midcourt, and the Warriors called a timeout with 0.9 seconds remaining. But the Warriors had already used all their timeouts. The technical foul gave Toronto one free throw and possession of the ball. Leonard hit the free throw, then drew a foul and hit two more from the line, and the Raptors had a 114–110 victory.

Leonard stood near center court with his arms raised as his teammates swarmed him. Moments later he accepted his second Finals MVP trophy. More importantly, the NBA title was heading north of the border for the first time in league history.

TORONTO RAPTORS
SPALDING
NBA
TM
© 1994 NBAP

CHAPTER TWO

WE THE NORTH

The Toronto Raptors joined the NBA as an expansion team in 1995. They entered the league the same year as the Vancouver Grizzlies, making them the first NBA teams located in Canada since the late 1940s.

After being awarded a franchise in 1993, the owners of the team set out to find a good nickname. They initially considered "Huskies," which would have been a nod to an earlier team that played in Toronto. However, the owners had a hard time coming up with a logo that was different enough from the Minnesota Timberwolves.

Instead, they came up with an unusual but memorable name. "Raptors" was one of three finalists that emerged from a nationwide contest. The name comes from the velociraptor, a dinosaur that was a key figure in the wildly popular 1993

Raptors vice president Isiah Thomas bursts through a banner featuring the team's logo at a press conference in 1994.

movie *Jurassic Park.* Team owners chose a cartoon dinosaur and a purple-and-red color scheme.

The Raptors hired former Detroit Pistons great Isiah Thomas as their first general manager. Thomas then hired former Pistons assistant Brendan Malone as the team's first head coach. Neither man lasted long in Toronto. Malone was fired after the team went 21–61 in its inaugural season. Thomas resigned in November 1997 after Toronto started the season 1–9.

A TASTE OF SUCCESS

Toronto's first four seasons were rough. A 30–52 finish in 1996–97 was Toronto's best record in that span. But the Raptors' fortunes changed in their fifth season. Toronto won 45 games and earned the sixth seed in the Eastern Conference playoffs. Though it was swept by the New York Knicks in the first round, the team seemingly had turned a corner.

With dynamic guard Vince Carter leading the way, the Raptors made the playoffs the next two seasons as well.

They even upset the Knicks in five games in the opening round in 2001. The series came down to a do-or-die Game 5 at New York's famed Madison Square Garden. Toronto won 93–89. Then the Raptors took the Philadelphia 76ers to seven games. Toronto bowed out only when Carter missed a long jumper at the buzzer in Game 7.

Vince Carter, *right*, fires a jump shot against the New York Knicks during the 2001 playoffs.

That run of success lasted just three seasons. Injuries led to losses, and losses led to frustration. In December 2004, the Raptors shipped Carter to the New Jersey Nets for a package of three players and two first-round draft picks. Two seasons later, they were back in the playoffs. NBA Coach of the Year Sam Mitchell guided Toronto to 47 wins and its first Atlantic Division title. However, Carter and the Nets knocked the Raptors out of the playoffs in the first round.

Toronto reached the postseason again the next year but once again failed to win a series. Soon the Raptors were back on the outside looking in. They missed the playoffs for five straight seasons. They also lost another star player in 2010. Forward Chris Bosh left for the Miami Heat. There he joined LeBron James and Dwyane Wade to form the backbone of two NBA championship teams.

REBUILDING AGAIN

The Raptors fell to 22–60 in their first year without Bosh. However, slowly but surely, they began to work their way back up in the standings. Finally, in 2013–14, they were ready for prime time. Fifth-year guard DeMar DeRozan earned his first All-Star appearance. Veteran point guard Kyle Lowry and small forward Rudy Gay were also scoring threats. Under head coach Dwane Casey, the Raptors won 48 games and the Atlantic Division title. It was just their second division crown in 19 years as a team.

That was the start of something big in Toronto. The Raptors ended up winning their division six times in seven years. But playoff success was a bit harder to come by. However, after losing in the first round two straight years, the 2015–16 Raptors went on the team's first lengthy playoff run. Seeded second

DeMar DeRozan (10) set a new career high by averaging 27.3 points per game for the Raptors in 2016–17.

in the East after winning 56 games, Toronto won seven-game series over Indiana and Miami before running out of gas in the conference finals. The Raptors fell to the eventual NBA champion Cleveland Cavaliers and James in six games.

TITLE TIME

Now that the Raptors and their fans had a taste of playoff success, they wanted more. They won first-round series in each of the next two seasons. But the Cavaliers swept them in the second round both years. Losing to James and the Cavs three straight seasons showed Toronto's front office that it needed to upgrade the roster if the Raptors were going to advance further.

Kawhi Leonard, *left*, soars for a contested dunk against the Cleveland Cavaliers.

In July 2018, Toronto made a risky trade. It sent DeRozan to the San Antonio Spurs for forward Kawhi Leonard. DeRozan was a quality NBA player and beloved in Toronto. In return, the Raptors were getting an incredible scorer and defender in Leonard. But he was in the final year of his contract. He could leave as a free agent after the season. The Raptors had one year to convince Leonard he could win in Toronto.

It turned out to be quite a year. The Raptors finished second in the Eastern Conference with 58 wins. Leonard and

Lowry represented the team at the All-Star Game. And they went on an epic playoff run, winning their first NBA title with a six-game victory over Golden State.

The risk had paid off, as Leonard helped them win a championship. But the superstar left Toronto anyway. Leonard signed as a free agent with the Los Angeles Clippers in the summer of 2019.

Raptors point guard Fred VanVleet, *right*, made his first All-Star team in 2021–22.

Over the next few years, other stars like Lowry also left the team. But Pascal Siakam and Fred VanVleet remained. Both players emerged as All-Stars. By 2021–22 Toronto was reloaded with a young, talented roster around the two players. After a slow start, the Raptors went 34–17 over the final few months of the season to reach the playoffs once again. Fans of Canada's only NBA team hoped it would be enough to vault Toronto back to the top of the league.

CHAPTER THREE

TORONTO'S HEROES

As excited as Toronto basketball fans must have been to get an NBA team, many were unhappy with the Raptors' first draft pick. The team used the seventh pick in the 1995 NBA Draft to select University of Arizona point guard Damon Stoudamire. Fans who had gathered in Toronto for a draft party booed the selection. They had hoped the Raptors would use the pick on UCLA forward Ed O'Bannon. The forward was the college player of the year after leading the Bruins to the national title that spring.

Stoudamire turned out to be the right choice. He started 70 games in his first year and averaged 19.0 points and 9.3 assists per game. That earned him the NBA Rookie of the Year Award. Stoudamire spent another 1 1/2 productive seasons in Toronto before the Raptors traded him to the Portland Trail Blazers.

Center Marcus Camby was the second pick in the 1996 draft, but the Raptors traded him after just two seasons.

That started a trend of top draft picks leaving Toronto before they could fully blossom. The team's top pick in 1996 was center Marcus Camby. An outstanding defender, Camby led the NBA with 3.7 blocks per game in his second season. Then he was gone, traded to the New York Knicks.

In 1997 the Raptors used the ninth pick of the first round on high school forward Tracy McGrady. Toronto eased the 18-year-old into the mix. By his third year, the athletic swingman was averaging 15.4 points and 6.3 rebounds per game. But McGrady made it clear he had no interest in staying in Toronto. The Raptors were forced to trade him. They shipped him to the Orlando Magic for a first-round draft pick. He immediately became a fixture in the Magic lineup and appeared in the All-Star Game the next seven seasons.

Vince Carter averaged at least 20 points per game in five of his six full seasons with the Raptors.

VINSANITY

The first true star developed by the Raptors was McGrady's cousin, Vince Carter. He arrived in Toronto through a draft-day trade that saw the Raptors and Golden State Warriors exchange picks.

The 6-foot-6-inch Carter was an instant hit in Toronto. He started all but one game his first season. That year he was named NBA Rookie of the Year after averaging 18.3 points per game. The flashy swingman made the first of 10 straight All-Star game appearances in his second season. Carter's sky-high vertical leap and elite quickness allowed him to get to the hoop and throw down highlight-reel dunks. He also developed into a deadly outside shooter. Carter hit nearly 40 percent of his three-pointers during his time in Toronto.

Sturdy power forward Antonio Davis arrived in a trade with the Indiana Pacers in 1999. He'd been a part of five Pacers playoff teams. The savvy veteran was never a big scorer. But his rebounding and leadership helped the Raptors reach the playoffs in each of his first three seasons with the team. Davis was also one of the NBA's most durable players. He missed only 12 games in those three seasons.

BOSH AND BARGNANI

After a miserable 2002–03 season, the Raptors earned the number four pick in the next draft. They selected 19-year-old Chris Bosh, a springy 6-foot-11 forward from Georgia Tech. Like Carter, Bosh earned a starting spot as a rookie and didn't take long to get comfortable at the NBA level. He made his first All-Star team in his third NBA season. He reached the midseason showcase four more times with Toronto. During that stretch, Bosh averaged 22.8 points and 9.9 rebounds.

Chris Bosh (4) swats a shot by Boston's Paul Pierce (34).

However, he made the playoffs only twice before famously leaving Toronto for the Miami Heat in 2010.

Toronto brought in another big man after they won the 2006 draft lottery. The Raptors used the number one overall pick on Andrea Bargnani, a 7-footer from Italy. Bargnani was more accustomed to playing a European style, where big men were expected to run the floor and shoot from the perimeter. He was never a big rebounder, but he made up for it with strong three-point shooting. Bargnani stayed in Toronto for seven seasons before the Raptors traded him to the Knicks.

Kyle Lowry, *left*, and DeMar DeRozan, *right*, helped the Raptors start a run of seven straight playoff appearances starting in 2013–14.

TITLE PIECES

Kyle Lowry was already a six-year NBA veteran when he arrived in Toronto before the 2012–13 season. He had never been an All-Star, and he had averaged double digits in scoring only twice. But Lowry turned out to be just the player the Raptors needed. His steady all-around game paced the team to its first five 50-win seasons. "Mr. Raptor" left the team in 2021 as the franchise's all-time leader in triple-doubles. And the league took notice of his skills. Lowry was a six-time All-Star with the Raptors.

Lowry's first year in Toronto was also the rookie season of center Jonas Valančiūnas. The hulking Lithuanian was a steady inside scorer and rebounder. The lineup was rounded out by 6-foot-6-inch slasher DeMar DeRozan. He was drafted in 2009 but truly blossomed in 2013–14. That year DeRozan averaged 22.7 points per game. That season also saw the team make its first of seven consecutive playoff runs.

However, neither Valančiūnas nor DeRozan were around when that playoff success turned into a title in 2019. Both players left in trades that directly contributed to Toronto's championship season. Valančiūnas even started 2018–19 on the Raptors' roster. He was traded to the Memphis Grizzlies in February 2019 as part of a deal for burly center Marc Gasol. The 6-foot-11-inch Gasol started all 24 playoff games that spring.

It was the acquisition of Kawhi Leonard that finally gave the Raptors exactly what they needed. He averaged 26.6 points and 7.3 rebounds per game. Leonard also was the guy his teammates turned to in the clutch over and over again as they pushed for the title. He was a second-team All-NBA and second-team All-Defensive pick during the regular season. Then he was named MVP of the NBA Finals after the Raptors knocked off Golden State.

SUPERFAN

Throughout the history of the Toronto Raptors, one fan has been a constant presence. Nav Bhatia was born in New Delhi, India, in 1951. Just over three decades later, he escaped the country after riots targeted members of his religion, Sikhism. He emigrated to Toronto in 1984. After initially struggling to find work as an engineer, often due to religious discrimination, Bhatia landed a job as a car salesman. His success in the field led him to become one of Ontario's wealthiest automobile dealership owners by 1995.

That same year, he became one of the Raptors' first season-ticket holders. Bhatia did not miss a home game until the COVID-19 pandemic forced all fans out of arenas in 2020. Along the way, he became known as the Raptors Superfan.

As his notoriety grew, Bhatia formed the Superfan Foundation to assist underprivileged children in playing

basketball. He has often paid for fans from across Canada to attend Raptors games. When Toronto won the NBA title in 2019, Bhatia became the first NBA fan ever to receive a championship ring. A year later, Bhatia was one of the first fans to be featured in a new fan-specific exhibit at the Naismith Memorial Basketball Hall of Fame.

Bhatia missed attending the game on December 10, 2021, after he tested positive for COVID-19 and was forced to isolate. It was the first time he had ever not attended a Raptors home game that held fans. Actor Kal Penn, who was in the middle of playing Bhatia in a film about the fan's life, went in his place.

CHAPTER FOUR

TORONTO'S TOP MOMENTS

On March 24, 1996, the Chicago Bulls brought an impressive 60–7 record to Toronto to face the expansion Raptors. Chicago was on its way to an NBA record with 72 wins in the regular season. The Raptors were 17–49. They had also won just three of their previous 18 games.

The Raptors played their first few seasons in the spacious SkyDome, Toronto's baseball stadium. That made for some huge crowds, especially when superstars such as Michael Jordan came to town. More than 36,000 fans came out on a Sunday afternoon to watch Toronto's newest team take on Jordan, Scottie Pippen, and the Bulls.

According to Bulls forward John Salley, the team held a party the night before and didn't take the game seriously enough. The Raptors made them pay. The home team took a five-point lead after the first quarter and led 56–54 at halftime.

Point guard Damon Stoudamire's team-high 30 points led the lowly Raptors to an unlikely victory against the Chicago Bulls in 1996.

"I remember thinking, 'How are we losing to these cats?'" said Salley. The 10-year veteran had started the season with the Raptors. But he asked to be waived so he could sign with a team that had a chance to win a title. Now he was getting an earful from his former teammates. "I kept pleading, 'We can't lose to these guys, please!'" he recalled.

Toronto's Oliver Miller hit a late free throw to give the Raptors a 109–108 lead. The Bulls had the ball for the last shot. With Jordan covered, long-range sharpshooter Steve Kerr fired a three-pointer that bounced off the rim. Jordan tracked down the rebound, turned, and launched a high-arcing shot that kissed the backboard and dropped through the hoop. However, his shot came just after the final buzzer had sounded. The Raptors escaped with a remarkable win, giving the Bulls their most unlikely defeat that year.

SLAM SAVER

The NBA held its first Slam Dunk Contest at the 1984 All-Star Game, and it was a huge hit. Some of the league's biggest stars would participate in the years that followed. Jordan, Dominique Wilkins, and Kobe Bryant were among the future Hall of Famers to win the title.

However, by 2000, the Slam Dunk Contest was losing steam. Top players stopped participating. They preferred to save their energy for the games that counted in the standings. In 1998

Vince Carter's gravity-defying dunks in 2000 helped make the NBA Slam Dunk Contest a must-see event again.

the league replaced it with a shooting contest with players from the NBA and Women's National Basketball Association (WNBA). The 1999 All-Star Game was canceled as the start of the regular season was delayed by a labor conflict between the owners and players.

Carter hangs on the rim by his elbow during the 2001 NBA Slam Dunk Contest.

By the time Toronto's Vince Carter took the floor in Oakland for the 2000 Slam Dunk Contest, it had been three years since the event had been held. He might not have realized it, but the future of the contest was on the line. As NBA executive Rod Thorn later recalled, "There was conversation that all the dunks that could be done had been done and maybe it was getting a little stale."

To help save the event, the NBA convinced some of the league's brightest young stars to participate. Carter, his cousin and Toronto teammate Tracy McGrady, and Houston guard Steve Francis were part of the six-man field.

Carter showed right away that he was serious about winning. His first dunk was a thunderous 360-degree reverse windmill. The fans, as well as Carter's amazed fellow All-Stars, couldn't believe what they'd just seen. As the cheers rained down on the court, the judges awarded the dunk a perfect score of 50.

His second dunk was another windmill that started behind the basket and ended with him facing the hoop. It earned "only" a 49. That was enough to clinch a spot in the finals alongside McGrady and Francis. But his final dunk of the first round might have been his best. McGrady bounced the ball high near the hoop. Carter leaped to grab it at its peak, passed the ball between his legs, and slammed it home in one motion.

Again, the crowd went crazy. A camera was focused on Carter. He looked squarely at it and waved his arms, mouthing, "It's over." Another score of 50 put him in first place heading to the finals. A buzz filled the arena as fans and players wondered what Carter might do next. It turned out to be a dunk that appeared to be rather basic, until it was clear what his freakish athletic ability had allowed him to do.

Carter approached the hoop from the right and took off. He kept soaring higher and higher with the ball in his right hand far above the rim. He threw it down and then hung on the rim to show that he'd put his entire right forearm—up to the elbow—through the hoop as he dunked the ball.

"I was quiet. I couldn't believe I just saw that," Francis said. "I don't think anybody in the arena knew what to think when that happened."

The stunned crowd soon began to appreciate what they'd just seen. They also knew the rest of the event was unnecessary. Carter had already won. But there was still more entertainment. For his final dunk, Carter sprinted the length of the court, took off just inside the free-throw line, and threw down a two-handed slam.

Carter had won the Slam Dunk Contest. But more importantly, he had saved the Slam Dunk Contest.

Carter (15) averaged 27.3 points per game during Toronto's 2001 playoff run.

THIS ONE COUNTS

Carter also played a huge role in the Raptors' first playoff series victory in 2001. A year earlier, they had suffered a three-game sweep at the hands of the New York Knicks. But a rematch in 2001 gave the Raptors a chance for revenge.

New York opened at home with a seven-point win. But the Raptors took Game 2 by 20 points to even the series. It was the team's first-ever playoff win. Back in Toronto, the veteran Knicks won Game 3 97–89. In a five-game series, Toronto was now one loss from elimination.

Instead, Carter's 32 points led the way to a 100–93 victory. The series went back to New York for Game 5. It turned out to be no contest. Toronto took the lead during a 14–2 run in the second quarter and never looked back. Former Knicks forward Charles Oakley hit a pair of free throws with 5.2 seconds left to seal a 93–86 victory.

The Raptors weren't satisfied with winning just one series, however. Next, they faced the top-seeded Philadelphia 76ers. The series promised to be a high-scoring shootout between Carter and Philadelphia's Allen Iverson. The 76ers point guard won the NBA scoring title and MVP Award that year.

Fans got exactly what they paid for. Iverson scored 54 points in a Game 2 victory that evened the series 1–1. Carter dropped 50 on the Sixers in a 102–78 rout in Game 3. But Iverson responded with 30 in a Game 4 win and 52 more as Philadelphia won Game 5 121–88.

Carter wasn't done, though. Back in Toronto for Game 6, "Vinsanity" returned as Carter poured in 39 in a 12-point win. That forced a do-or-die Game 7 back in Philadelphia. Perhaps worn out from their duel, Iverson scored just 21 points while

Carter slipped to 20. Trailing by a point in the final seconds, the Raptors' star missed a 19-foot jumper. The Sixers escaped with a hard-fought series victory.

SHOOTER'S BOUNCE

The Raptors won the 2019 NBA title with a six-game victory over the Golden State Warriors. But they wouldn't have survived to face the Warriors if not for one of the most memorable last-second shots in NBA playoff history.

Toronto faced Philadelphia in the second round of the Eastern Conference playoffs. They split the first six games. Game 7 was in Toronto. Just as in 2001, the teams went down to the final seconds. Philadelphia forward Jimmy Butler's basket with four seconds to play tied the score 90–90.

After a timeout, the Raptors inbounded from midcourt. Everyone in the arena knew Toronto would try to get the ball

Leonard Leads the Way

After Kawhi Leonard's dramatic buzzer-beater against Philadelphia, the Raptors quickly got into trouble in the Eastern Conference finals. The Milwaukee Bucks won the first two games. Game 3 in Toronto turned into an epic, double-overtime battle. Once again it was Leonard who turned things around for the Raptors. He played 52 minutes and led Toronto with 36 points. The Raptors outlasted the Bucks 118–112 and swept the rest of the series.

Kawhi Leonard is mobbed by teammates after hitting his buzzer-beating shot against the Philadelphia 76ers in 2019.

to Kawhi Leonard. The team's star forward had already scored 39 points on the day. So, it was no surprise when he received the pass at the top of the key. Guarded closely by defensive ace Ben Simmons, Leonard dribbled to his right. Philadelphia center Joel Embiid stepped up to double-team him. Leonard raced past him to the corner of the court, where he launched an off-balance jumper over the 7-foot Embiid as the clock ran down.

Leonard posed in the corner with his right arm held high, his hand in a perfect shooter's follow-through. The ball struck the front rim and bounced up again. Leonard went into a crouch position, willing the ball to roll in. The ball bounced twice more as time seemed to stop. It finally settled through the hoop.

Leonard was mobbed by his teammates. One month later, he was mobbed again as he accepted the NBA Finals MVP trophy. Leonard had come up with many big moments during Toronto's magical run. But none was bigger than the first Game 7 buzzer-beater in NBA history.

TIMELINE

1995

The NBA expands to 29 teams, adding two new franchises in Canada, the Toronto Raptors and Vancouver Grizzlies.

1996

The Raptors go 21–61 in their first season but earn the distinction of handing the champion Chicago Bulls one of their 10 regular-season defeats that year.

2000

Vince Carter wins the NBA Slam Dunk Contest, then leads the Raptors to their first playoff appearance.

2001

Toronto defeats the New York Knicks in the first round of the Eastern Conference playoffs before falling to the Philadelphia 76ers in the second round.

2004

The Raptors trade Carter to the New Jersey Nets on December 17.

2007

Toronto wins its first division title, and Sam Mitchell is named NBA Coach of the Year after leading the Raptors to a 47–35 record.

2014

Third-year coach Dwane Casey and the Raptors win the first of three straight division titles, but they bow out in the playoffs in the first round.

2016

The Raptors win their first playoff series in 15 years when they beat the Indiana Pacers in seven games. They also knock off the Miami Heat before falling to the Cleveland Cavaliers in six games in the Eastern Conference finals.

2018

After being swept by the Cavaliers in the playoffs for the second straight year, the Raptors trade star guard DeMar DeRozan to San Antonio for veteran forward Kawhi Leonard.

2019

The Raptors go on a memorable playoff run, defeating the Golden State Warriors in six games to win the NBA title. Leonard leaves that summer as a free agent.

2020

The Raptors reach the playoffs for the seventh consecutive season but fall in the second round.

2021

"Mr. Raptor" Kyle Lowry leaves to join the Miami Heat. Pascal Siakam and Fred VanVleet step into leadership roles.

FRANCHISE HISTORY
Toronto Raptors (1995–)

NBA CHAMPIONSHIPS
2019

KEY PLAYERS
Andrea Bargnani (2006–13)
Chris Bosh (2003–10)
Vince Carter (1998–2004)
Antonio Davis
  (1999–2003, 2006)
DeMar DeRozan (2009–18)
Serge Ibaka (2017–20)
Kyle Lowry (2012–21)
Tracy McGrady (1997–2000)
Pascal Siakam (2016–)
Damon Stoudamire (1995–98)
Jonas Valančiūnas (2012–19)
Fred VanVleet (2016–)

KEY COACHES
Dwane Casey (2011–18)
Sam Mitchell (2004–08)
Nick Nurse (2018–)

HOME ARENAS
SkyDome (1995–99)
Scotiabank Arena (1999–)
  Formerly known as:
  Air Canada Centre
  (1999–2018)
Amalie Arena (Tampa)
  (2020–21)

TEAM
TRIVIA

CELEBRITY FAN

Toronto-based musician Drake has officially been a "global ambassador" for the Raptors since 2013. He's partnered with the team on several promotional campaigns and is often seen courtside at Raptors games.

THE FRIENDLY PURPLE DINOSAURS

The Raptors caught some flak for their early uniform and mascot choices. Their purple jerseys with a dinosaur on the front were dubbed by critics their "Barney uniforms," after the purple dinosaur from children's TV fame.

FANCY COLOR

The Raptors named their shade of silver "Naismith silver" to honor James Naismith. The inventor of basketball was born in Almonte, Ontario, which is 230 miles (370 km) outside of Toronto.

TAMPA RAPTORS?

Travel restrictions imposed by the COVID-19 pandemic made it impossible for players to move freely between the United States and Canada during the 2020–21 season. As a result, the Raptors were forced to play their home games in the United States. They spent that season playing in Tampa's Amalie Arena. The Raptors went 16–20 in their "home" games but finished out of the playoffs.

GLOSSARY

alley-oop
A pass that is caught and immediately dunked before the shooter lands on the ground.

assist
A pass that leads directly to a basket.

clutch
An important or pressure-packed situation.

draft
A system that allows teams to acquire new players coming into a league.

durable
Tough and long-lasting.

expansion
The addition of new teams to increase the size of a league.

franchise
A sports organization, including the top-level team and all minor league affiliates.

free agent
A player whose rights are not owned by any team.

inaugural
Marking the beginning of an institution.

layup
A shot made from close to the basket; an easy shot.

rebound
To catch the ball after a shot has been missed.

rookie
A professional athlete in his or her first year of competition.

triple-double
Accumulating 10 or more of three certain statistics in a game.

BOOKS

Flynn, Brendan. *The NBA Encyclopedia for Kids*. Minneapolis, MN: Abdo Publishing, 2022.

Graves, Will. *NBA*. Minneapolis, MN: Abdo Publishing, 2021.

Mason, Tyler. *Ultimate NBA Road Trip*. Minneapolis, MN: Abdo Publishing, 2019.

ONLINE RESOURCES

To learn more about the Toronto Raptors, please visit **abdobooklinks.com** or scan this QR code. These links are routinely monitored and updated to provide the most current information available.

INDEX

ABOUT THE AUTHOR

Patrick Donnelly is a freelance writer who lives in Minneapolis, Minnesota. He has covered the NBA for 20 years.